and

Stuck in the Tree

'Seeds' and 'Stuck in the Tree'
An original concept by Jenny Jinks

Illustrated by Kathryn Selbert

Published by MAVERICK ARTS PUBLISHING LTD

Studio 3A, City Business Centre, 6 Brighton Road,

Horsham, West Sussex, RH13 5BB

+44 (0)1403 256941

A CIP catalogue record for this book is available at the British Library.

ISBN 978-1-84886-289-0

Maverick
arts publishing
www.maverickbooks.co.uk

This book is rated as: Red Band (Guided Reading)
This story is decodable at Letters and Sounds Phase 2.

Seeds
and
Stuck in the Tree

By Jenny Jinks

Illustrated by
Kathryn Selbert

The Letter P

Trace the lower and upper case letter with a finger. Sound out the letter.

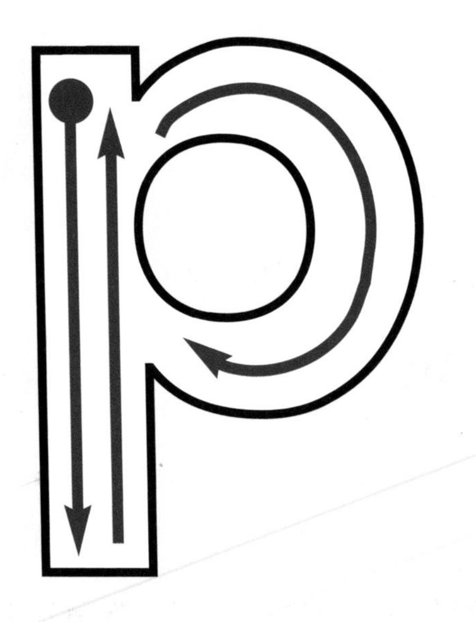

Down,
up,
around

Down,
up,
around

Some words to familiarise:

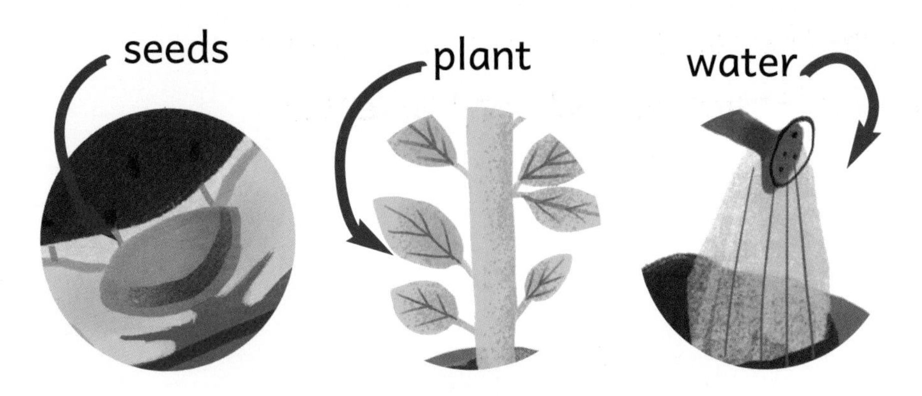

High-frequency words:

is go in the a on no

Tips for Reading 'Seeds'

- Practise the words listed above before reading the story.

- If the reader struggles with any of the other words, ask them to look for sounds they know in the word. Encourage them to sound out the words and help them read the words if necessary.

- After reading the story, ask the reader what Tim and Pip's seeds grew into.

Fun Activity

Plant carrot or sunflower seeds of your own.

Seeds

Tim is big.

Pip is not.

Tim and Pip get some seeds.

Tim's seed is big.

Pip's seed is not.

Tim and Pip get big pots.

The seeds go in the pot.

Tim and Pip water the seeds.

Tim tips in a lot.

Pip tips in a bit.

Tim and Pip check on the plants.

Tim's plant is big.

Pip's plant is not.

This plant is the best!

Tim and Pip love their plants.

The Letter K

Trace the lower and upper case letter with a finger. Sound out the letter.

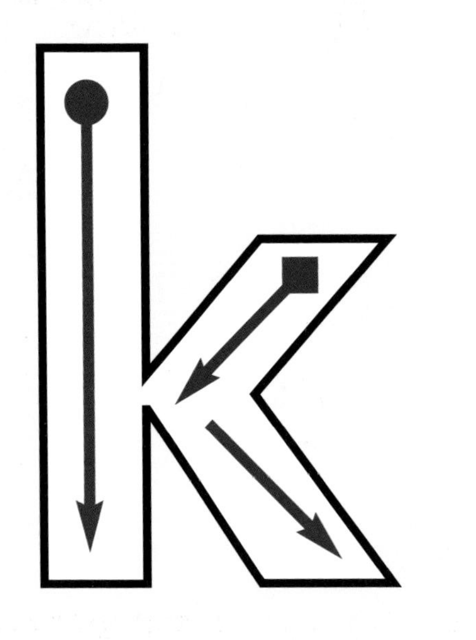

Down,
lift,
down,
down

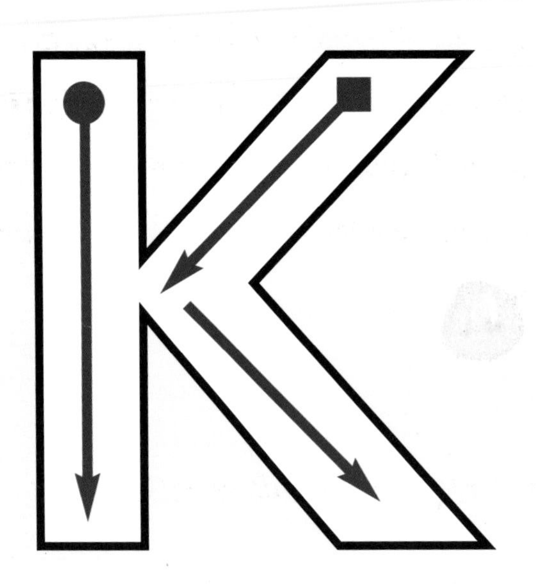

Down,
lift,
down,
down

Some words to familiarise:

High-frequency words:

is in the said are they a up

Tips for Reading 'Stuck in the Tree'

- Practise the words listed above before reading the story.

- If the reader struggles with any of the other words, ask them to look for sounds they know in the word. Encourage them to sound out the words and help them read the words if necessary.

- After reading the story, ask the reader if they remember who was stuck in the tree.

Fun Activity

Ask the reader how they would get down if they were stuck in a tree.

Stuck in the Tree

Kit is in the tree.

"Get down," says Dad.

But Kit is stuck.

Dad climbs the tree.

Now Kit and Dad
are in the tree.

"Get down," says Ben.
But they are stuck.

Ben climbs the tree.

Now Kit and Dad and
Ben are in the tree.

"Get down," says Mum.
But they are stuck.

Mum gets a ladder.

Ben and Dad climb down,
but Kit cannot.

Mum climbs up.

Kit jumps down.

Mum is in the tree.

Book Bands for Guided Reading

The Institute of Education book banding system is a scale of colours that reflects the various levels of reading difficulty. The bands are assigned by taking into account the content, the language style, the layout and phonics.

Maverick Early Readers are a bright, attractive range of books covering the pink to purple bands. All of these books have been book banded for guided reading to the industry standard and edited by a leading educational consultant.

For more titles visit:
www.maverickbooks.co.uk/early-readers

Pink

Red

Yellow

Blue

Green

Orange

Turquoise

Purple

Title	ISBN
Dog in a Dress and Run, Tom, Run!	978-1-84886-290-6
Buzz and Jump! Jump!	978-1-84886-250-0
Bam-Boo and I Wish	978-1-84886-251-7
Sam the Star and Clown Fun!	978-1-84886-288-3
Seeds and Stuck in the Tree	978-1-84886-289-0